NOW and FOREVER

Life - where are we going

Bob Ede

Poems by
Anne Ede

Grosvenor House
Publishing Limited

This book is published by
Grosvenor House Publishing Ltd
Link House
140 The Broadway, Tolworth, Surrey, KT6 7HT.
www.grosvenorhousepublishing.co.uk

A CIP record for this book
is available from the British Library

ISBN 978-1-83975-577-4

Contents

Contents

1. Now And Forever

'Now and Forever' is an understanding of life and death based on love being the meaning and purpose of life.

The 'now' being explained in poetry by Anne Ede – her poems being taken from her acclaimed, by all who read them, book *'Now and Then'*, published by Grosvenor House Publishing Ltd.

The text being written by Bob Ede for the 'forever' part, from his understanding of life and death after a lifetime following Jesus Christ, which has brought him joy and happiness, and a lot more besides.

Anne Ede experienced commercial life in London before devoting her life to her family with three children, and others, becoming a Director and Company Secretary of the family business later on. Her hobby was writing and publishing poetry, which expressed herself.

Bob Ede was trained as a voluntary Youth Worker by the Surrey County Council and holds a degree in Applied Christian Theology from the University of Kent. He studied counselling at the London

School of Theology and was instructed by SE Coast Ambulance Service paramedics as a Community First Responder. Qualified as a plastics technologist, his career was in sales and marketing.

Both have been members of St John the Baptist Church, Wateringbury, Kent for more than 40 years.

This book is offered in the hope that it will give some simple, and lovely, acceptable answers to those who seek a meaning and purpose to life itself, or to those who just want to reconfirm their faith, as they did themselves.

Crossroads

Lord, I need your guidance, Lord, I need your hand
For I'm standing at a crossroads and I do not understand
Why you sent me down a pathway where the signposts
    seemed so clear
But in the end it petered out and now I've come back here -
Fretting – Is it this way? Is it that way? Which way should
    I go?
And my mind is in a turmoil and I really do not know …….
Yes, I know that I should listen, but your voice just isn't clear

And the more and more I struggle the less and less
    I hear.
Now the dawn is hardly breaking and my head is spinning
    round
As I clutch at straws that pass me but they flutter to the
    ground -
And I ………………………

"Peace …….peace…….Be still ………….be still…………
Breathe deeply now, relax your will,
Empty your mind of all that disturbs you:
Just repeat "Lord, Lord" - I *have* heard you.
Try not to rush, try not to hurry,
There is plenty of time and no need to worry.

Wait – no – just wait, accept and believe,
The choice will come clear in a day – in a year -
You need hope, you need love, I have hold of your hand,
Just remember I really do understand.

And when you can trust and have no more fear
One night a voice will come clear in your ear:
'*There* is your path – *there* is your way'
Then just get up and go, there's no need to stay.
Now follow the Spirit, follow the Light
And, yes, laugh aloud – the future is bright!"

Problems

Dear Lord,
I have some problems – things of real concern,
Enough to wake me up at night and make me toss and turn.
Then my mind begins to fret and my thoughts go round and
    round,
And I plot and plan and worry but an answer can't be found.
Should I speak out or stay silent? Be brave or turn away?
Will the mountains of the night become molehills in the day?
Would silence bring solution or courage promote peace -
Please help me find the answer so these wearing worries
    cease.
For I know if I can truly trust my problems to your hand,
You will point me in the way to go and help me understand.

Guardian Angels

Do angels slide down a sunbeam,
Can they swing from a shooting star,
Do they scatter moon-dust in children's dreams
And smile on them from afar?

Do angels wrap wings around you,
Hold your hand when you're feeling sad,
Do they breathe sweet peace into hardened hearts
And sing to make you feel glad?

Do we each have our own special angel -
One who guides us when life goes all wrong,
Who never rests in their mission
To return us to where we belong?

2. Who Am I?

Humans are super brained animals who differ uniquely from other animals because they have the power to reason as opposed to living by instinct; although scientists have been trying to disprove this with the training of chimpanzees for many years, unsuccessfully. Products of devolution, humans came out of Africa 1.8 million years ago when, as tree living creatures, they came down and started to walk as the 'homo erectus' species. Their brains rapidly developed since the Ice Age some 14 thousand years ago to its present-day maximum capability.

Just living forces humans to make choices and reason how they are going to meet those choices.

"What am I going to eat today, and how am I going to get it?"

People may also ask themselves, "What am I doing here on earth and what is to become of me?" is the natural instinct of self-preservation. Other animals just go out by instinct and forage.

In reasoning, an answer to this dilemma "who am I?" it is natural to seek 'pointers' to try and to make a conclusion, studying not only nature's birth and death but also the magnitude of the universe, which only adds to the question of "why?"

Studying history of why some believed in God, or gods, should give a lead to enable one to form one's own ideas, but believing in spirituality and the afterlife, is not only incredulous but also, without proof, unbelievable. However in history and today, people do claim to have been radically 'changed' by a religious experience to transform themselves from an ordinary person to a loving person. With an illogical lifestyle of excessive giving to others of money, time and actual love, and worshipping, again with love, with the hope of an eternal life – but confirming their beliefs with only joy and happiness!

But where is the proof to all of this? Because it is all illogical to the intelligent person who demands proof and who rejects the whole idea of spirituality as just wishful thinking.

History tells us in the Bible that, to some, God's enormous power lies in His ability to 'change' people so that they emerge from this experience with a 'meaning and purpose' in life, their questions about life answered.

But what is this 'change' by God that it is claimed by millions to have changed their lives totally, either slowly to a point of sudden conclusion or dramatically? This 'change' is not a simple signing up to belong now to the 'Christian Party' but a total, even to death, commitment to 'Love God and others', and history is littered with those who have died for the cause; from Christ to St Stephen, to modern day Dietrich Bonhoeffer and many others who were burnt at the stake. Spirituality is more powerful than life itself and God's power to change people to this extent is convincing proof of His existence.

Yet why do the majority reject and deny the very existence of God? Today, prosperity and good education has bred in us a belief in ourselves alone to not only control our lives but to be self-sufficient. Third-world countries are more religious than the West, but interestingly the USA, the 'land of individual opportunity and capitalism', is the most religious country in the West. And, in the middle economies, religion survived to prosper decades of communism, particularly in Russia, which opposed it.

But we have to ask, "Why does God want us to change? Are we not doing okay as we are and we are happy as we are?"

God is Love, which we know to be true because 'we feel His love' when we communicate with Him. He answers our prayers and we acknowledge He gives us so many blessings. And we feel His constant presence; always ready to listen to us and inspire us. In fact, we would do none of the illogical things we do in love if we were not inspired by God to do 'the right thing', to be the kind of people He wanted to create; people who loved God and others naturally and all the time. Perfect people as an objective within their God given self-will. But, if the message is not clear, or if one questions it, it can be checked by us asking ourselves, "Would Jesus Christ have done this?"

Love is defined as a 'very special feeling'. It traverses time and space and God, being the centre of love, is the reason that many hope to go there on death, meeting God as Christ historically promised.

Loving God is no different from truly loving a person – courting with gifts and communication, wanting to be with them in presence, helping, giving up time and say money, admiring and worshipping, and loving forever. And like with a person getting joy and happiness from the relationship, and the hope of eternity, no guarantee, only the hope and, certainly is no reward, for just loving God and others because it is the right thing to do. However, trusting Christ to lead you to God is a different matter.

In conclusion as to, "Who am I?" I am an intelligent animal who is alive by chance with the sole purpose of living an enjoyable life whilst helping others and being a nice person because that is who I am. Alternatively, I can seek a higher purpose in life and from the history of people who have found a spiritual life with enough meaning for them to commit to it by changing their lifestyle, beliefs and meaning and purpose in life, with the hope of getting joy and happiness and everlasting love. Hoping that this will extend into eternity.

Remember This

When you wake up in the morning
And don't want to start the day;
When your problems press upon you
And you can't push them away -
Remember this:
God Loves You.

When each little task seems pointless
And you're tired beyond belief;
When each leaded limb is lifeless
And you cannot find relief -
Remember this:
God Loves You.

When there's no light round the corner
But a vice around your head;
And you cry and cry for nothing
Even wish that you were dead -
Remember this:
God Loves You.

When you're driven down upon your knees
In an agony unknown;
When there's no-one who will understand
And you feel you're quite alone -
Remember this:
God Loves You.

When resentments crowd in on you
And despair defeats you still;
When you're moved to shout "God help me" -
Remember this:
He *will!*

Free Gifts

It's a dark day: let the sunshine in -
Think of rainbows, think of robins,
Think of cats purring;
Think of daffodils and snowdrops -
Spring's new life stirring.

It's a dull day: let the sunlight in -
Think of ploughed fields, think of new leaves,
Think of cuckoos calling;
Think of apple trees and bonfires -
Autumn's colours falling.

It's a dismal day: let the sunbeams in -
Think of sea-spray, think of pebbles,
Think of crabs scurrying;
Think of silver fish and rockpools -
Oceans hundreds hurrying.

It's a dark day: let God's light shine in -
Think of Jesus, think of comfort,
Think of peace descending;
Think of prayers said and answered -
God's love unending.

Looking at "The Light of the World"

A strong but loving face,
A firm but gentle hand,
A light that always shows the way
And eyes that understand.

He waits upon your doorstep,
He knocks upon your door,
He hopes that He can enter in
So you need search no more.

Count Your Blessings

Gaze at the sky on a frosty night
How many stars are shining so bright?
Peer in a pool on a summer's day
How many fish are swimming your way?
Kneel on the beach and scoop up the sand
How many grains do you hold in your hand?
Pick up a sunflower and shake it around
How many seeds will fall to the ground?
Lie in your bed in the early morn
How many songbirds will welcome the dawn?
Stroll through the spring-time and you'll be surprised
How many colours will gladden your eyes.
Now count all your blessings
How many you'll find
To lighten your heart and freshen your mind.
And never forget when your counting is through
To send God a loud and joyful "Thank you"!

Thank You

"Thank you" is such a little phrase
We use each day in many ways:-
Thank you for the cup of tea,
The bubble bath you gave to me;
Thank you for my annual rise;
Thanks for baking apple pies;
Thank you for the sound advice -
And all the times you've been so nice.
Thank you, postman, for the letter;
Thank you, doc, I'm feeling better.
Thank you, Dad, for seaside fun,
For touchline cheers until we won!
Thank you, Mum, for cleaning, shopping,
Washing, ironing, never stopping.
Thank you, sister, thank you, brother,
For laughs we share with one another.
Thanks my friend for being there -
The lovely flowers to show you care.
And thank you, thank you Lord above
For never failing in your love.

3. Where Are We Going?

Tony Hancock, the brilliant radio and TV comedian of the 1960s, had a sketch in which he, sitting on a London-bound commuter train, said out loud his depressed thoughts about life, "where are we going?" Only to be answered by the man seated opposite, "Waterloo."

This brief look at life perhaps illustrates how we all, at some time or another, wonder just what we are doing with the answer being something mundane and beyond our control, like earning a living. Thinking that life must have a greater purpose and reason than just existing, living and dying – but what? Think on, maybe. Or as Tony Hancock, again said in another sketch, "Or shall I go to the cinema?"

Time is always in short supply, especially when there are so many more enjoyable pastimes than spending it thinking about life. It is therefore hoped, and thought, that these reasonings may be of interest to those who lead busy lives, but nevertheless have the same questions as most about the meaning and purpose of life. And, although not all will agree, they are thoughts that, if time permitted, would have been considered before maybe dismissing them if you were to end up with a considered opinion of your own.

It has been quoted as a fact that everyone has prayed if only once in their lives, but not all have repeated it – probably because it was not successful in producing the result that was wanted. But, then to pray for a 98-year-old dying man to live was hardly likely to anyway! Whereas peace might have been – but would not this have the outcome anyway? Maybe not.

These are the type of questions of life we all toy with, if we are to recognise that humans are the only species in the world who have the power to reason. All other animals do things by instinct. These reasoned thoughts are recorded for those who want to know more and perhaps want to challenge those who claim to be too intelligent just to believe as some do. But, for those who want just a simple faith, the poems of Anne Ede are included, which perhaps illustrate the peace of a simple faith without the need to challenge or debate.

4. A Relationship With God

The question often asked is, "How do I become a Christian and believe in God?"

The answer usually being, "You just pray, and keep praying until you get an answer. You will be moved in some way, be it a feeling or some motivation and, if you don't, seek help because this could be the beginning of your real life forever."

Establishing a relationship with God through prayer is the first step to changing from an ordinary person to an illogical and irrational person who is inspired and motivated by God to do things way above their natural ability and confidence levels in the name of love.

It proves that there is a God because He changes people to give them faith, love and hope – enough for them even to die for, as many have!

Change can come instantly and dramatically like St Paul on the road to Damascus, or slowly after years of study and discussion. The time of realisation that you now know God personally sometimes results in your punching the air in a eureka moment of exciting discovery.

The start of a relationship with God may begin slowly at say, Sunday school, school or a youth organisation, or later in life when you feel that life must have a greater meaning and purpose than just living and dying; especially, if the premature death of yourself or a loved one is threatening. It does not matter the reason. What is important is that life will have a real meaning and purpose, which is to have a relationship with God who created us and the universe.

Prayer is the foundation of believing in God, who in spirit is always there to inspire, help and guide you. A typical quick prayer being, "Lord, if I fall from this ladder, please catch me," with the reply received through the mind, "No, I do not do physical things, tie the ladder on." Or, on hearing an ambulance siren, "Lord, guide the crew with their skills." The crew may not purposely hear God – but you would have cared and done your best in love.

A relationship with God becomes wanting to please Him, as the creator of the universe and you, in particular, because a relationship with God is a personal one. Pleasing God is trying to do His Will – loving God and all others – trying to be perfect and getting joy and happiness from what you are doing, which one hopes will last forever into eternity. But to be perfect is impossible because there are too many temptations on earth and people continually sin, often unintentionally, and maybe only in a small way. However, God's greatest gift to us was in Jesus Christ dying to pardon such sins to make us acceptably perfect for eternity.

Traditionally it was always 'sins' that got in the way of a relationship with God. With the sacrifices of the most perfect birds and animals available being made to give God back something in atonement, which was regarded as very precious – a life.

John the Baptist, who was a Levitical Jewish Priest, on account of his father also being a Priest tracing his ancestry back to Aaron, introduced mass atonement of sins, with baptism in the River Jordan. The 'washing away of sins for forgiveness' so that a good relationship with God may continue without the necessity of killings. Jesus Christ surrendered his life as a sacrifice for everyone in the whole world who wanted forgiveness for their sins throughout their lives, in order to keep their relationship with God strong. Baptism today is taken as perfectness at the time before usually being welcomed into church membership.

Being inspired by God to do illogical and irrational things above one's own natural ability for love of others and doing it for others without any personal reward to you, or even your family, is committing oneself to God. Be it joining a group in the voluntary service of others, giving money, running a youth organisation, loving and helping others, or just praying. And, without personal reward in some way, would be seen by many as pointless unless you had a relationship with God. Yet people devote their lives to what is called 'serving God', which is the reality of God.

When one starts a relationship with God, heaven is usually not a consideration as one's current life is all that is important at the time, although it becomes a consideration as time goes by. For if one's Christian life gives you happiness, love, joy and a meaning and purpose in life, you will want it to spiritually go on forever – forever into eternity – as God promised through Jesus Christ.

Having a faith is actually experiencing God's love through prayer, meditation and inspiration.

Nature gave us life, but God's love gave us the opportunity of a life with meaning, purpose and a future. It is sad when people just live and die, which as the Beatles song said, 'All You Need is Love' to become part of creation 'now and forever'.

5. Let's Not Talk About It

Since the reign of Elizabeth I, Christianity has been England's state religion, Elizabeth making herself Head of the Church of England and Head of the English Government, with independence and defined roles for each. Today, about 500 years later, the situation remains the same but with less of the population now being committed Christians and an even larger body opposing the very existence of a God. Although it is interesting that on survey the majority of people, when asked, especially on hospital admission forms, to 'state religion' appear to play safe and put 'C of E'. Showing perhaps that there is something there that has not been, but possibly maybe, developed.

What is apparent is just how strongly people feel about the subject. So much so that, along with politics, it is commonplace that the subject is barred amongst friends from the social dinner table; which is strange as there is no other subject that is as important as life and death, and this perhaps indicates a fear of the inevitable?

To the non-believer, being a Christian is nonsensical and a result, in many cases, of childhood brainwashing and wishful thinking, of 'make believe'. Many are annoyed, and even cross, that people assume that they 'live on a higher spiritual plane than them', as if they have a higher intellect and know something that the others don't. It is not surprising that what starts as a discussion leads quickly to argument with neither side willing to concede because it is a subject of such consequences and is therefore best ignored.

What is the Christian argument to justify their fanciful, unproven, illogical and irrelevant belief in spirituality and the afterlife, if it is not just to be 'wishful thinking' with a total and unnecessary interference in their social life and even standard of living?

Christians would claim:

- A personal relationship with God (and what could be greater?), with constant help to do the 'right' thing.
- Security, with a constant 'presence' to help and advise.
- A discipline, that helps keep us out of trouble, which is appreciated and, importantly, a meaning and purpose in life – not just existing – with an eternity of God's personal love, encouraging us to love Him and others.
- Joy and happiness of knowing of God's love, doing His Will.

All this is, of course, dependent on there being a God, which is proven by the fact that He constantly intervenes in the lives of millions of people, the rich and poor, the famous and ordinary, the weak and the strong, to totally change them from being just people to loving and caring people as the priority of their lives; changing to live illogical lives loving God and others. It simply does not make sense if it were not for the joy and happiness the Christian receives experiencing God's Power of Love when one totally changes and commits oneself to God.

Changing for most people is a dramatic experience, whether it comes at the end of a long period of study or a sudden revelation, but it is usually when one seeks God's real help for the first time. Not just prayers for the family but, "Lord help me – I need your help now!"

And the response is felt, as an answer in itself, "I am here, and I will never leave you."

It is an answer of love; love, as with human love, being a very special feeling, a feeling that you would possibly die for, although in practice many have.

Seeking God's love for yourself is natural; we all want to be loved and give love in a special relationship. But God's love is fought against by many for the fear of what they might be letting themselves in for, certainly the loss of independence, control and self-esteem. Besides, people just do not believe, it is all too incredulous for an intelligent person. However, to deny God's proven existence is committing to a life of absolute nothingness, just an existence, to be forgotten within a few years as a person, with perhaps only recorded achievements being of historical value.

What we would all agree however is that the world is full of power, magnificence, mightiness and is organised. Science tells us that nothing comes from nothing. It is therefore not arguable that the world cannot be without reason for its creation. Jesus Christ, who demonstrated that he had mysterious power, and was God's 'being' on Earth, explained some of God's power with His statement, "In my Father's house there are many rooms." Solid reasons for some to put their trust in God but to others to say, "All make-believe. Let's not spoil the meal by arguing."

6. Love

The greatest privilege ever is to be invited to love God and humanity and have a worthwhile life, with an everlasting future.

Love is the purpose of life around which everything is centred and is spiritual. True love is empathy where you feel the pain or distress of the one you love, or the others you love. It is being in their shoes and you feel what they feel. True love is spiritual empathy.

Hence, when God created humans, He gave them the emotion of love. Not only for personal advantage but to share generously with time, money, passion and empathy with all other of God's human creations. To be selfish with God's gift of love would be unappreciative of our own creation.

The message from God is simple – love others and God, and your life will not have been in vain as you will have contributed to making the world a far, far better place. But how important is it that you know that God loves you regardless? Not at all, say some, because we do not believe in God or His, so called, blessings. Like the beauty of the setting of the sun, which we have enjoyed anyway.

True, but to know that the blessing came from God is to know that God loves you personally and is as important as getting a bunch of flowers from someone you know rather than anonymously. Most blessings, gifts from God, are just there anyway – God or no God – but to be able to speak to God and be guided by Him, is a blessing which is personal to you, for it makes you important in the world having a very special relationship. It makes your life worthwhile and gives you a meaning and purpose in life.

Most importantly, one can appreciate all of nature's being as gifts or blessings from God which all contribute to the person you are; a person loved by God who speaks to you, and guides you, and shows His love for you with the blessings He personally gives you – some available to all anonymously, but you personally.

Speaking to God, usually in prayer, is not a listing of requirements, however much needed, but showing empathetic feeling for others, feeling for their pain and distress, and for yourself. Prayer is not for God's physical action – people do that for God who is loving Spirit – prayer is for inspiration for you or someone.

If one is praying routinely it can be boring. Like, say, praying for 'good Government' rather than a particular action which is meaningful to you personally, making prayer itself more meaningful. Remembering, of course, that one is praying for someone to be inspired to do something and one will always be dependent on the person responding.

God's constant presence ensures that we are never alone, and He is there always ready to listen, even in death with the fear of the unknown. As Cliff Richard said to David Frost, a TV presenter, in answer to a challenge, "What if God doesn't exist?"

"But, what if He does?" retorted Cliff.

Love is spirit and has no boundaries or time limitations. Hence, you can love a person near or far who you might never see again, or if dead their spirit – who they were. Similarly, you can love God for His blessings, His love for the world and giving us Jesus Christ, the greatest blessing of all. Jesus who carries not only God's love but ours and those we love because love is what we have in common with him.

Practicing Christians love Jesus Christ. They remember his dying for their forgiveness by symbolically eating and drinking his body and blood, and for this they love him. They also love him for giving them a real life of joy, happiness and purpose, as well as a future in eternity.

Showing them, and teaching them, how to love God and humanity.

As with humans, Jesus Christ's spiritual love is communicated through his face, the expression, the eyes, the half-smile, the lips and the concentration. People express their love back by focusing on Jesus' face and reading it, be it from a statue, icon, painting or in their minds. The face portraying love. A deep and sincere love which often brings tears of emotion because of the power of such love.

Loving, and being loved, spiritually and empathetically, and for eternity, is what the world is all about. Without spiritual love life would be totally meaningless.

Does one have a reason or purpose for being on Earth if it is not to love God for our being? To take full advantage of God's love will make one the wonderful person we all hope to be.

Interval

There's times when I just need to *be*
Not fret and fume but wait and see
What plans God has in store for me.

There's times when I just need to gaze,
Not dash and rush but stand amazed
By beauty that's enfolding me.

There's times when I just need to hear -
Not talk and talk – and never fear
The silence that can speak to me.

There's times when I just need a space,
Not work or friends but peace and grace
To find the Lord who loves me.

Love

Consider these:-

Sparkling dews,
Rainbow hues,
Mountains grave and grand,
The oceans deep
Where dolphins leap,
A baby's curling hand.
Soft rounded hills,
Gold daffodils,
A freshly furrowed field,
The raindrops' beads
On myriad seeds
Their hidden life to yield.
Misty dawns,
Summer lawns,
The elephant's wise old eye,
Musicians' hands,
Physicians' plans,
The flaming sunset sky.
And wonder:-

Do all these things a lifetime brings
Just randomly appear?
Is a perfect plan
Too vast for man
Most surely working here?
Stand quiet .... be still .....
Relax your will
Feel the Spirit moving deep,

The pulse that beats
Through skies and streets,
Worlds waking and asleep.
A mind so wise,
An arm so strong
To guide, to teach, to tend -
The Spirit moves,
The Spirit serves
And loves us to the end.

7. Making A Difference

Leaving the world a better place than when one entered it must be the aim of everyone who value their lives as important – 'their' being just as important as people who have position and power. For it is the small grains of sand that make the magnificence of the beach.

We all know, because it has been said so many times, that when love conquers the world there will be peace amongst the nations and, just as importantly, peace amongst people.

Yet is this ever likely to happen? We have to hope that it will and, in the meantime, all play our little bit towards it, even though we are just a grain of sand – but a very important grain of sand, like all grains of sand.

Promoting love in the world, silently and often without recognition, is powerful in its own small way, however small, as it sets an example for others to follow if they can see the effect it makes and they question the motives; the answers often completing a 'jigsaw puzzle' of exploration into their own meaning and purpose of their life.

Little acts of love are seen constantly inside, say, a church or a village hall community, where acts of greeting and helping others is commonplace, but outside such a community it is more difficult, apart from fundraising for worthy causes, as this is often seen as interference – especially if done by the church. Hence, a lot of loving organisations are officially secular, although sometimes run by people of faith doing their own thing.

Where Christian people show love for others, in a silent and unrecognised way, is in prayer. Praying for someone in need shows your love, which is generated from empathetic care and interest in them and your desire to give the help that they need. The help and need which are often beyond your ability to do practically but with your belief that the spiritual help you can ask God to inspire in them will give them the peace, calmness and genuine hope that God is with them at that moment of crises.

Such prayers are not just for the war-torn areas where our empathy should make us feel the pain of the victims, and fighters, regardless of fault, but also for people like the lonely who can be desperate, and many others. For them all to know that somewhere, someone is praying for them must raise their spirits.

Of course, people can reject our prayers, they can refuse God's inspiration 'to do the right thing' and go their own way, and not be inspired by God's presence. But, you would have done your best, the only thing you could have done. You would have cared for them and showed empathy for them. You would have felt for them, and they would not have been alone – God would have been by their side as you had asked him.

God is the creator, He is Spirit, He does not do physical things, He inspires us to do them for Him. To love others and to be kind to them, and to pray for His Spiritual love for all of us in need.

8. Promises

The most significant event ever in the world was when God promised life forever to everyone who had faith in, and believed in, Jesus Christ, who became Saviour of the World. Urging, and showing, people how to love God and their neighbours as the way to the Kingdom of Heaven.

> "For God so loved the world that He gave Jesus Christ, for whoever has faith and believes in him, will live forever in the eternity of Heaven" *(Adaption John 3:16.)*

The state of heaven being supported by the magnitude, vastness, and complexity of the universe and the outer space which is beyond measurement.

We know that we will all soon die, and our bodies perish – that is nature and is okay, it has to be. But do we want our inner selves, our spirit of loving relationships, which bring us so much joy and happiness, and justifies our living, to die with our body? Those who want their spiritual lives of relationships and love to live on forever will do, because Jesus Christ promised it.

Jesus said:

"I am with you always to the end of time" (*Matthew 28:20*).

"I am the way. No one comes to the Father except by me" (*John 14:16*).

"In my father's house there are many rooms. If it were not so would I have not told you that I go now to prepare a place for you" *(John 12:2)*.

"If you really know me then you know my Father as well" *(John 12:7)*.

"Peace I leave with you – my peace I give you. I do not give as the world gives. Do not let your hearts be troubled and do not be afraid" *(John 14:27)*.

"Father, I desire those who are your gift, may be with me where I am, so that they may look upon my glory. The love thou hast for me shall be in them and I may be in them" *(John 17:24)*.

"Sir. We sat at your table and you taught in our streets. And, He will say I tell you, I do not know you. Out of my sight all of you and your wicked ways" *(Luke 13:26)*.

"Come all you who are weary, and I will give you rest" *(Matthew 11:28)*.

"Everyone who has faith in him (Jesus Christ) may not die but have eternal life" *(John 3:15)*.

"But the unbeliever has already been judged" *(John 3:18)*.

In Answer to a Question

When I was a child I thought as a child
And my faith was simple and strong;
I knew God was there to watch over me,
To guide me when I went wrong.

Every night I would pray for the poor and the sick
And for those who could not see,
For my mother on earth, for my father in heaven,
And I also prayed for me!

But "when you are grown", the Gospel says,
You must "put away childish things":
So I delved and denied and unsettled myself
With the doubt that questioning brings.

Is it fair that I'm rich when others are poor?
That I'm happy when others are sad?
That there's sickness and grief and war in the world
Inner turmoil that drives men mad?

How can God allow children to suffer and die
While evil men flourish and grow?
And why all the wars that senselessly kill,
Ruin lives, flatten lands in their throe?

But is it God's will or is it men's sin
That wreaks this grief on the earth?
And didn't Christ die to offer us life,
Rise up to give us new birth?

As time has gone by I've come to believe
That God always answers our prayer -
Even buried so deep that we scarcely knew
The prayer had been rising there.

The answers are not always quick and clear,
Or what we wanted to hear -
But be patient and wait and you will find
Your troubles will disappear ....

Not disappear in the practical sense -
You must work not take your ease -
But deep in your heart you know you're at rest
Your inner-most self is at peace.

And as for the world that's outside ourselves -
If each of us only saw
The presence of God in everything
Maybe we'd search no more.

For He's there in the beauty, the colours, the sounds
Of the mountains, the sea and the sky,
And also in poverty, pain and neglect
As for these Christ suffered and died.

For God asks that we suffer nothing at all
That Christ did not suffer before;
If we trust there is deep overwhelming love
And compassion we cannot ignore.

For "Come unto Me" Lord Jesus says,
"And I will give you rest".
And, if you do, you'll have found a friend -
The One who will stand any test.

What Can I Do?

What can I do? What can I say
To make myself useful in some small way.
I sit in this chair day in day out -
I can't do the cooking, I can't get about.

I have someone to shop and someone to clean,
And someone to start my washing machine;
The ironing is done, I'm given a bath,
The weeds are pulled up in the garden path.

Not long ago I was needed by all -
I would cheerfully help whatever the call,
But now I feel useless, finished and sad -
Tell me what can I do to make someone glad?

What opportunity? What are you saying?
That I really can help people by praying?
Well …. maybe you're right and maybe it's true -
At least it would give me something to do.

And, yes, I could pray for my neighbours and friends,
And strength for my children whatever God sends.
For all the world's problems, for those in despair,
For the sick and the prisoners, for all those who care.
So then when I'm asked what I do all day
I can simply reply: "I love – and I pray".

9. Heaven

When we die, as we all most certainly will, what will we have to look forward to in order to happily go without regret for what we are leaving behind?

Going to Heaven is not the purpose of life. The purpose of life is for all people to love God and humanity, says Jesus Christ, who proved his authority by his miracles and unquestionable philosophy. Heaven is for those who have dedicated their lives, at some stage, to following Jesus Christ's teachings and want to take their love to God forever.

Because heaven is a mystery it is ignored by most and accepted by some as just a wonderful place of peace and worship where God resides. Attractive to the avid church goer, being taken on faith, and desirable to some others as an alternative to nothingness. It is, maybe, nevertheless feared by all, who recognise it as an unknown and unchartered territory, which requires from them their maximum faith and trust.

We know that God exists because we not only communicate with him both ways and He inspires us. We also know that He actually changes us and people beyond their former recognition of themselves. We know also that Jesus Christ speaks the truth, which was reported by not just one but by many. His legitimacy and authority being proved by not only his miracles, but also by his perfect, unquestionable philosophy.

Trusting with faith, therefore that Heaven exists, we have to ask what are our expectations of Heaven? And, do we really want to go there, especially when we are told that we will be judged and possibly be cast aside if not worthy?

Would it not be safer to just go to sleep and call our life well lived and complete?

So, what do we really want from an afterlife in Heaven?

We do not know what heaven means for sure but have hopes that it will reflect the reality of our lives on earth in abstract perfection. With the hope of:

> *Peace* – from constant pressures and decisions in life.
> *Rest* – from weary struggles to just keep on going.
> *Freedom* – without any responsibilities.
> *Beauty* – as in life but now in perfection.
> *Painless* – after much pain.
> *Companionship* – with those we have loved, there or within our hearts.

Timeless – unlimited just to think of good and nice things.
Isolation – from tragedy.
Finalisation – no fear or doubt of the future.
Love – unlimited love, giving and receiving.

Knowing God now in Glory, Splendour and Worship, and being part of His fantastic creation – such will be an indescribable experience.

Meeting and relating to Jesus Christ will be amazing – such power, such love, such gentleness – the perfect person in every way.

Feeling happy and content recalling our efforts doing God's Will and knowing with satisfaction that we did not waste our life.

Knowing and perhaps recalling all our sins have been forgiven, will make us happy.

Simply put – if we have loved our Christian life, whatever the difficulties, we will want to live forever, but in Heaven.

For those who have difficulty in 'belief' – especially in their being a Heaven – do not even try, just know that God loves you, and that this love is for 'now and forever', and that death is no barrier to His continuing love.

Heaven is for all who follow Jesus Christ, and for those who do not, and are loved by those who do, they will be with us in our hearts forever. Because It would not be heaven for us who loved them if they were not. Loved ones become part of our spirit.

When we die, we must die happy, happy with the spiritual empathetic love we have given, or tried to give. Be content and satisfied that we have also done our best, in the circumstances. Now at peace as the 'job' is done, and at rest from the effort of life. Excited that we will meet our maker and longing to meet our friend Jesus Christ. Relieved that Jesus Christ will be with us on the final part of our journey. Happy to be 'home' with all those who we love – FOREVER.

10. Conclusion

God constantly inspires us to do the right thing. In loving God and Jesus Christ, we experience joy and happiness which lasts forever, even after death. This gives us a meaning and purpose in life, rather than just an existence.

Many want nothing more which is okay, but we are glad that we have the choice. To leave the World on death, being led by Jesus Christ to God, with no regrets, should put a smile on our faces. Knowing that in our short life we have done our best to do what was right – loving God and humanity. Our having no doubts or fears about the future as we will be with God, as Now and Forever.

So, this is where we are going – not Waterloo!

The Lord's Prayer

Our Father...

"Our Father " sing the birds
As they soar above the breeze,
"Our Father mouth the fishes
As they swirl beneath the seas,
"Our Father" trumpet elephants
While they crash through jungles deep,
"Our Father" squeak the dormice
As they curl their paws in sleep.
"Our Father" sighs the west wind
While it breathes on vale and hill,
"Our Father" shrieks the hurricane -
His might prevaileth still.
Our Father strong, unchanging,
The mountain crags proclaim,
Our Father deep, eternal
Vast valleys praise His name.
Our father sends the seasons,
Old English oaks rejoice,
Our Father gives us new life -
Sweet snowdrop's spring-time voice.

So help us then, our Father,
In all creation see
Your wondrous hand is working
For all who worship Thee;
And in Your love unchanging
With all earth we are blessed
As we kneel to pray "Our Father"
And in Your arms we rest.

Who Art in Heaven

Who can imagine the wonder of heaven-
The breadth, the depth, the height,
The sweetness as the angels sing
Forever in God's sight.

Who can imagine the peace that's in heaven -
Soft wings, strong arms, God's grace,
The joy of those who now behold
Christ's tender, loving face.

Who can imagine the love that's in heaven -
The glow, the warmth, the flame,
Of those who kneel before God's throne
And praise His glorious name.

And yet if we can truly seek
That wonder, peace and love
We'll find on earth, within our hearts,
Our God from heaven above.

Hallowed Be Thy Name

Beasts of burden, soaring birds,
Weeping willows, grazing herds,
Massive mountains, crashing seas,
Bustling beetles, towering trees -
In their being worship You.

War-worn women waiting, dry,
Still small children starving, cry,
Brown-eyed babies staring, plead,
Wizened ancients, crouched in need -
In their suffering worship You.

Sounding trumpets, pianos playing,
Choirs singing, dancers swaying,
Painters' colours, writers' stories,
Craftsmen's visions, sportsmen's glories -
In their joy worship You.

In churches splendid, chapels bare,
Stifling rules or free pure air,
In soul-less halls or rooms alone,
With vibrant song or prayers unknown -
In our faith we worship You.

Thy Kingdom Come, Thy Will be Done on Earth as it is in Heaven

Within our hearts there is a way
To build God's Kingdom here each day:
If we could learn to live in peace
And, trusting Him, let doubting cease,
If we could forward look with hope,
Despair would drown and we could cope
With all this life's complexities.

If we could just hold out a hand
The pain in others understand;
If we could in our hearts forgive,
Anger would fade and we could live
To bridge the world's injustices.

If we could give, not count the cost,
To those whose happiness is lost
Then we would build our lives on love
And with the help of God above
Show heaven's possibilities.

So help us then, dear Lord, we pray
To build your Kingdom here each day.

Give Us this Day our Daily Bread

In this land of plenty the bread we need is love
The food we need is Spirit poured out from God above.
Love divine to nourish our hard and hungry hearts,
Spirit of God to enter our souls so dry and parched.

But in those lands so needy for bread their hands reach out,
For water pure and plenty their shrunken bodies shout.
Yet there they suffer silent; they never think to hate,
With deep, accepting Spirit for love they watch and wait.

Forgive Us Our Trespasses

Forgive me, Lord ....for what, this week?
I know I should forgiveness seek
But when I think of what I've done:
I really cannot think of one sin I've committed!

I've done no murder, told no lies,
Not coveted my neighbours' wives,
I've never stolen, do not swear:
So really cannot think that there is one sin I've committed!

I've phoned my parents once or twice
And helped some people - been quite nice,
I've prayed in church and so I'm sure
There really are not any more sins I've not committed!

....

My child, look deep into your heart and you will surely see
The things that you would *not* have done had you truly
    followed Me!
Has your tongue lashed out in temper? Is your spirit full of
    pride?
Has contempt for other people been such you could not
    hide?
Do you judge by what is outward, not search the inner man?

Do you neglect your neighbour or help them when you can?
Can you accept your problems and turn from them with
    hope
Or wallow in self-pity: are convinced you cannot cope?

Could you be so self-absorbed in the good you feel you do
That the worth that dwells in others is overlooked by you?

But remember …..
If these words strike cords within you then hold fast to
    My peace -
For I've promised you forgiveness and a love that will
    not cease.

As We Forgive Those Who Trespass Against Us

Buried deep they rise unbidden
Those wrongs that have been done -
Unforgotten, unforgiven,
They grow and linger on.

The smallest slights, a silly saying,
Harmful hurts, a wicked word,
Never silenced, ever-present,
Angry whispers always heard.

Lord You have forgiven me
The wrongs that I have done -
Eased my sadness, healed my wounding
The pain I felt now gone.

So I must no harbour hatred,
Must forget not just forgive,
Only then will Your peace find me
Only then be free to live.

Lead Us Not into Temptation

Dear Lord,
Please keep me safe, please hold my hand,
Please guide me on Your way.
Please guard my tongue, please cleanse my thoughts,
Please show me when I stray.
Please quench my pride, please make me meek,
Please purify each day.
Please give me strength, please show me joy,
Please drive the dark away.

But Deliver Us from Evil

Please help me always look to You
When I am worn and weak,
Please let Your light shine forth to give
The peace I always seek.
Please let me never be deceived
By evil's tempting ways,
Please show me how to lean on You
On dark depressing days.

And with Your help I know that I can seek to do Your will
And when I falter You will guide and bless and love me still.

The Kingdom, The Power and The Glory

For Yours is the Kingdom we all hope to find
Your power can make all things new
And Your glory that lasts for ever and ever
Will shine through the work that we do.

Lightning Source UK Ltd.
Milton Keynes UK
UKHW010743250721
387663UK00003B/139

9 781839 755774